MOON CREEK

T0159937

MOON CREEK

Seeking the secrets and beauty of this world through poems and images

SUSANNA ENSO HUANG

THE **BLACK SPRING**
PRESS GROUP

First published in 2023

Maida Vale Publishing
The Black Spring Press Group
Maida Vale, London w9
United Kingdom

The author has requested the publisher use American spelling
and grammar wherever possible in this edition

Illustrations by Katie Lu
Typeset by User Design, Illustration and Typesetting, uk
Cover art by Edwin Smet

isbn-13 978-1-915406-44-6

CONTENTS

Acknowledgements   137

For my daughter Katie,

You came with light, illuminating and warming my little world.
   I'm seeking the meaning and beauty of life, for myself and for you.

ABOUT ME

Moon Creek is a real little creek flowing behind
a stone house surrounded by pine trees.

During the pandemic, my scope of activities was
reduced to the village where I live. I often went out
for a walk, through the tree-line boulevard, towards
the tranquil pond in the woods.

I walked through Spring, Summer, Autumn,
and Winter. All my emotions, such as happiness,
sadness, disappointment etc., all dissipated during
the walks.

At work, my mind was running like a high-speed
machine.

While walking in the woods, I could hear my
inner voices singing in silence.

The mysterious veil of the World was lifted
before my eyes. Everything in front of my eyes was
so beautiful and fresh, like dewdrops on the small
red berries in the morning.

I saw   the ordinary flowers on the roadside
         gleaming in the Sun;
I saw   the branches of a big tree dancing excitedly
         in the storm;
I saw   a bird standing under the tree near the little
         pond in the rain;
I saw   the autumn leaves spreading out into
         a rainbow carpet;

I saw   a crystal snowflake shining in the snow;
I saw   the clouds changing into the shapes of
          dragon and phoenix;
I saw   the reflection of the setting Sun whispering
          to the small tranquil pond…

The emotions flowing from my heart day and night
have turned into the long and short sentences in this
Moon Creek poetry.

Since childhood, we have been taught how
to make a living, but seldom we do learn how
to **be happy**.

On a winter's day, I saw the laps of my daughter's
footprints on the small pond covered with ice
and snow. I realized that our happiness could be
lost unknowingly in the day-to-day "circle of
footprints" of making a living. If we could walk
back to the warm heart covered in "ice and snow",
we could meet happiness again.

Books have opened a wonderful spiritual
world for me one after another, warming me
and comforting me. My intention is very simple.
The World is so big, there will always be readers
who could see a small corner of the Magical World
through my eyes.

Maybe, you are sitting in front of the window
with a coffee in one hand and this book in another.

Maybe, you are lying comfortably on the green
grass, with this book spread in front of you.

For a moment, everything around quietly
disappears...

When you come out of the book, you may be able
    to see
the tiny little flowers on the side of the road in full
    bloom,
hear the birds sing over the treetops,
feel the breeze blowing across your cheeks,
and see the white clouds in the sky changing shapes.

This is Your Happiness. It is also My Happiness.
    I am grateful to meet Me in this book and meet
You in the Moon Creek.

STAR GATE

Will you
walk me into the silver star gate
waiting for the opening
of the flower stamens
in the golden light?

Will you
take me into the deep blue of night
over the silhouettes of trees
watching the bright Moon
in the infinite starry sky?

SPRING

PURPLE FLOWERS

Tiny little purple flowers
blooming in the dry leaves at the roadside, claim

"The Spring is here for us to see the World in
flowers."

A TINY LITTLE FLOWER

I have a tiny little flower
blossoming in my yard

Do you have a tiny little flower
blossoming in your heart?

PRAYING GIRL IN THE WOODS

The praying girl in the Woods listens
to the whispers of spring blossoming flowers

The praying girl in the Woods watches
the singing of flying summer cicadas

The praying girl in the Woods feels
the dancing of autumn falling leaves

The praying girl in the Woods remembers
the warmth of winter snowflakes

A FEATHER IN THE DREAM

A white feather was falling in my dream
saying hello to me in the morning breeze of spring

MOON & CLOUD

Moon gets up early
to play with the White Cloud
wondering if she falls
would she be caught
by the White Cloud?

CLOUD WHISPERS

Two white clouds
meet in the blue sky
whispering to each other
all day and all night

FLOATING

Her feelings are like the floating clouds
not knowing from where it comes
and not knowing to where it goes

GLOBE

We have only one Earth
floating in the vast Universe

DREAMY RIVER

The golden sun shines on the river
like a sweet dream
flowing through the mysterious rippling creek

AUSPICIOUS CLOUDS

Auspicious rainbow-colored clouds
appear in the blue sky
like a flying dragon and a dancing phoenix

BIRD WISDOM

I whisper to the big bird
standing still by the little pond

"What are you pondering
in this precious moment of the dawn?"

"Nothing, it is you who are pondering."

BLUE SKY IN EYES

Dyed with the azure blue starry sky
her eyes set out to seek wisdom and light

A SMALL TREE UNDER STARS

The azure blue sky
with one arm decorated with the Big Dipper
another the North Star
hugs the small tree
under the early summer starry night

DREAM

It was like a dream
Fairies were dancing
Parents were clapping
Happiness was spreading

It was like a dream
A sweet childhood dream

TEARDROP OF THE MOON

In the early morning
the Moon turns into a teardrop
slipping from the soft Sky's cheek before
freezing on a branch top

The Moon watches the smile of a scented flower
and listens to the whispers of the creek

TWO LEAVES

The Sky is clear
but the mist is still out there
Two leaves on a branch are ready to fly

LITTLE BIRD

Who are you waiting for,
little bird?

You paint yourself
in the blue sky

Would you like to sing alone
when all your friends have left
leaving you in the empty sky?

A FALLING LEAF

A curious bird ponders over
her best moment in life
not singing in the first ray of sunshine
not sleeping in the nest at night
but watching a falling leaf
dancing slowly in the soft sunlight

ROSE PETAL

I am searching for a place to write
Someday you may find and enjoy

Could it be on the petal of a yellow rose
If not on the grass or white clouds in the sky?

BIG ROSE AND LITTLE ROSE

On a stone wall climbed two roses
growing slowly at their own pace

Big rose whispers to little rose
"I will bloom first, waiting to see yours."

LIPSTICK

"Why do you apply lipstick of red?"
asked the inquisitive little boy of his sister

"Because it gives my plain lip the beauty
of a blossoming flower."

TWO TINY FLOWERS

Why are the two of you
not meeting each other on the treetop
while the warm breeze is blowing?

Why did the two of you
wait so long before falling onto a green leaf
into a teardrop gently swinging?

A RED FLOWER RING

Walking into the dark night
in the soft music of Moon Creek
her breath was taken away
by a shimmering red flower ring

SUMMER

NIGHT FLYING

Ride through the starry dark night
Wait in silence for the dawn
We will paint the cloudy sky with the Sun

PLAYFUL LIGHT

The light plays freely in the sky
under the white cloud's gentle care

She secretly paints the white clouds
with the splendor of golden light

JOURNEY OF LIGHT

Asked the girl to the light

"How many nights
did you take to fly across the dark sky
arriving at my windows
to watch the pink flower swaying
in the gentle waves of my smile?"

SMILE

Your smile
    flows into my heart
passing through my eyes
like a gentle breeze
kissing the grass,
trembling the blades

OLD VILLAGE

I invite you
to visit my old village

I ask you
to look at the direction of my finger

Could you see
a "goddess" in the clouds
also living in my old village?

SWORD DANCE OF FLOWERS

The morning Sun illuminates the leaves of green
A red cardinal sitting on a branch swing

He asked a white flower in the wind

"Dear fair lady as clean as ice and as pure as jade
are you walking into the early morning mist
to have your elegant sword dance in the wind?"

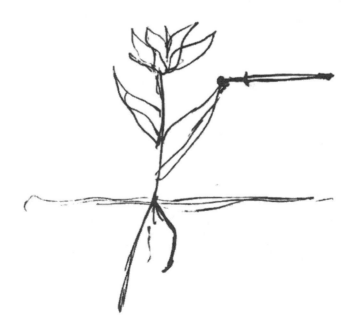

BEAUTY FAR AWAY

My heart touches the beauty far away
My soul wraps around her and carries her away

LITTLE BLUE FLOWER

I don't know your name
little flower

I see you as blue as sky
and you are a little shy

I don't need to know your name
little flower

I remember you as blue as sky
and you are a little shy

LITTLE DEER IN THE WOODS

Here comes a little deer from the woods
elegant, gentle, and dotted with the plum blossoms
embroidered by the lady when she was a child.

THE COLORS OF MORNING LIGHT

Do you want to pause your hurried steps?
Come with me to count the colors
of the morning light shining through green leaves

FLOWER AND FENCE

The fading crescent moon
does not want to depart
from the sky of blue

The blossoming red flower
wants to be in the same picture
as the fence of wood

A CORNER OF THE WORLD

Walking by the fragrances of roses
she could not bear the thought of plucking a rose
worrying a corner of the world would be sadly lost

SHADOW DANCE

The Shadow finds joy dancing with the Light
under the gaze of a Rose who nods her head

ROSES ON THE WOODEN FENCE

Two roses rest together
on the wooden fence
painted with the staff for the songs of summer
cicadas

Two roses rest together
in the gentle breeze
rippling through the grasses of various green shades

BIRD SHADOW

A bird enjoys dancing
in front of a tree
forgetting its shadow
when flying away

INK PAINTING

Walking through a small tunnel at night
she saw an ink painting on the starry sky
of the dark trees and bright stars at night

SEE AND HEAR

Could you
see her heart in the cloud?

Could you
hear her whisper in the wind?

LITTLE STONE GIRL

A little stone girl is happy
standing in the creek alone
watching the creek
flowing all the way to the sea of unknown
in the days of light
in the darkness of night

A LITTLE TREE

A little tree in our village
seeks to touch the white clouds

A tall tree painted by Van Gogh
longs to reach for the sky

DEER CHASING

A couple of deer enjoy playing together
chasing in the green woods

Why would they still want
to fight for the throne in central plains?

WATER LILIES OF MONET

The girl visited the Museum of Art in Autumn
to stand in front of the water lilies of Monet
studying the clouds and the sky
hidden in the strokes thick and light
and feeling the soul of Monet

The girl walks along the trails in summer
to stand in front of a small pond nearby
imagining the reflection of flowers under clouds
like the water lilies of Monet

BABY DUCKLINGS

Baby ducklings
swimming in the pond.

Where is your mom?
Where is your dad?

Where do you find
your peace of mind?

A WATER LILY

A water lily has a peaceful mind
leaning gently on a green leaf
in the shimmering pond

A water lily has a light heart
watching quietly the floating clouds
in the shimmering pond

LITTLE ANGEL

Little angel was in the sky
She lost a wing and could not fly

She watched the white snow melt
She watched the crescent moon shine
She watched the singing bird rest

Little angel is not in the sky

A TALL TREE

On a moonlit night
a tall tree reaches out to touch
the swirling starry sky
in the drifting flower scent
at the intersection of
infinite space and time

NIGHT SKY

My little world
is only one of the twinkling stars
in the boundless night sky

FAIRYTALE OF MOON AND STARS

On a summer's night
she enters the world of fairy tales
watching through the window
the dances of the moon with stars
in the dark blue starry night

LITTLE WHITE FLOWER

I think about you
A little flower
On the roadside

Your pure white petals
Your golden pollen-heart

When I pass by
You blossom alone
At the roadside

CLOUD OF FLYING HORSE

A flying horse
begs me to write
a poem for him
on his silver feather of light

WINGED HORSE

More than two thousand years ago
the winged terracotta horse
flew alongside the King of Qin
running tens of thousands of miles
His eyes were bright and wise

But the light in his eyes
dims with boredom and sadness
for he is honored with taking rest
in the soft music and dance
performed in faraway Hua-Qing Palace

FLYING HORSE

A free-spirited white horse
soars across the sky
to be with white clouds
where he was born in the light

LIGHT IN SKY

Bright moonlight
shines in the dark sky of blue
caressing my heart and
illuminating my long trip home

LITTLE GOLDEN FLOWER

Where did you shower
in the golden light
to greet me playfully
in the morning light?

A LITTLE LION IN THE WOODS

A ray of golden morning light
shines upon the little stone lion

He once lost his way in dark nights
but never lost his dreams
to explore the unknown sky

He waits until a ray of bright morning light
Shines upon him

A GIRL WALKING IN SUNSET

Walking into the afterglow of a beach sunset
the little girl is already in the place
of love and light
which she will seek in many other places

AUTUMN

STRAY BIRD

I see the Blue Ocean
in the sky

I see a Stray Bird fly
across the Blue Ocean Sky

I see the Little Me and Little You fly
riding the white clouds high
in the Blue Ocean
where the Stray Birds fly

RED AUTUMN LEAF

She asked the red leaf
lying on the pebbled road

"When did you fall quietly from the sky
to kiss our mother earth a last goodbye?"

LITTLE RED BERRIES

Little red berries
wearing morning dewdrops
are seen on the bushes
hanging above the green lawn fences

BIRD ON A FENCE

In the early autumn light
a bird dancing on the branches
puzzles over a question

"Who will teach me to sing,
insects, cicadas, or other birds?"

I WANT TO ADOPT A LITTLE DEER

I want to adopt a little deer
at Sunrise

I will set it free
on the misty green lawn

I want to adopt a little deer
in the Sunshine

I will let it wander
on the rainbow leaves lawn

I want to adopt a little deer
under the Sunset

I will bring it home
to sleep in its mom's soothing songs

DEER SMILES

My deer smiles at me in the woods
wearing the wreath of golden leaves

He throws a rock in my heart pond
watching the ripples in the oil painting of Autumn

TWIN DEER

Twin deer
are walking together

Twin deer
are running together

Twin deer
love playing together

Twin deer
are seeing the World together

LIGHT DANCE

Lights
dance, dance, dance
on the wall

Lights
dance, dance, dance
off the wall

Lights
dance, dance, dance
from my heart

Lights
dance, dance, dance
in your heart

WORLD IN A DEWDROP

The miracles of Heaven and Earth
are unveiled in the dewdrop of a poet's words

THE WORLD IS SHY

The World is shy
she is hiding her beauty in the veil of fog

The World is shy
she doesn't know her beauty in the veil of fog

The World is shy

TREE-LINED TRAILS

Autumn breeze blows
Autumn leaves fall
Autumn rain pours

Do you know how many rainbow colors
are hidden in the tree-lined trails?

WHITE MUSHROOM

A white mushroom petted by the green grass
imagines herself as a bright moon
hanging in the blue night sky

FLYING

A bird standing on a branch
unfolds its white crystal wings
ready to fly into the wind

CHOIR IN THE CREEK

Come to the choir
Soft music in the wind
sung by bird, creek
and wind chimes before rain

TRAIL

"The road is tortuous"
claims the shadow of a long trail fence

WAITING

What are you waiting for
standing in the splendor of Sunrise
in silence?

What are you waiting for
listening to the whisper of Wind
in silence?

COURAGE

Where could I find the precious courage
to walk into the mystic Unknown
in the rustling green forest
in the whisper of wind
in the dark tunnel
in the light
in me

LONELY LITTLE TREE

A lonely little tree
inserts her silver hairpin
onto the Sun before bed

A lonely little tree
asks the passing-by wind
to take off her yellowed leaves
piece by piece to the ground

FALLEN AUTUMN LEAVES

Watching the leaves
dancing in the autumn breeze
she whispers to herself,

"Better not to sweep the leaves away
from this colorful carpet in my way."

COLORS OF AUTUMN

One, two, three, four, five trees
picked their favorite colors to paint
on the sky blue of the pond in the wind

COLORFUL AUTUMN LEAVES

The colorful autumn leaves fly from the tree
to run away with the creek to the sea

STICK PICTURE

A girl draws a stick picture
by moving a few mountains
by building a few temples
by planting a few trees
by watching a few clouds,
in a village hidden in the green mountains

GEESE IN THE VILLAGE

Geese in the village
swim around in the pond
not willing to disclose any secrets
in their songs

RED LEAF

Sitting alone on the balcony
she has a glimpse of a red leaf
dancing with its shadow
in the beautiful melody

FOG

When the fog rises
she stands on the grass
looking back at her blurry memory
with no words

DEER IN THE FOG

I am searching for you,
my deer, in the fog

Yesterday, you were there
on the green grass
looking deep into my eyes

I am searching for you
my deer, in the fog

Today, you were not there
on the green grass
leaving emptiness in my eyes

WATER LILIES IN THE RAIN

She ran to the trees
standing by the pond

She watched the water lilies
blossoming in the rain on the pond

A LEAF IN THE RAIN

I walked in the rain
The sky is painted in grey

I saw a red leaf in the rain
It has a small hole inside its rim

I looked through this hole in the rain
Here is a teardrop of the moon in my dream

SMALL WOODEN HOUSE

The sound of autumn rain
blurs her vision
of the small wooden house
in the deep grass green

WATCH THE MOON

Watch the Moon
It changes its colors
It changes its shapes

Watch the Moon
I change its colors
I change its shapes

Watch the Moon, until
Your time freezes
Your space disappears

Watch the Moon
You change its colors
You change its shapes

THE MOON

She wakes up at night
She falls asleep at dawn
She only takes a nap
In the glow of the setting Sun

YELLOW ROSE AND HOURGLASS

How many particles of sand would slip
before a petal of my yellow rose falls

ART OF MEMORY

Last summer
Grandma wove several scarfs
long and short

On a snowy winter day
Granddaughter wrapped them
into a loving piece of art

SKY

When was the last time
You looked up at the sky

A white cloud rests there
waiting for the fallen Moon
to wipe her tears

When was the last time
You looked up at the sky

FALLING MOON

If the Moon falls
Do not feel sad
It will happily glide

I SEE POEMS...

I see poems hanging along with red berries
I see poems lying with fallen autumn leaves
I see poems playing with tender deer
I see poems singing with morning birds
I see poems flowing with the dancing creeks
I see poems twinkling in your lovely eyes

HUG

A lonely little tree
standing in the autumn wind
sighed into her bare branches
"I lost all my leaves."

A passing white cloud
hugs the little tree
whispering to him gently
"May I be your blossoming flowers?"

CANDLELIGHT

The candlelight looks at her reflection on the
window
imagining the dance of Sunlight and Moonlight
with soft music playing in the starry night

WINTER

ROSES IN SNOW

She carved her silent blessing
on the scent of a yellow rose

She froze it in the snowy ice
and delivered it in a mailvan of lights

She sent the scent of this yellow rose
traveling over half the earth
to melt in the warm sea breeze

LONELY WHITE SAIL

The lonely white sail
has not lost her direction
in the waves of the ocean

The lonely white sail
is waiting for the blowing wind
to show her direction again

BEACH HOUSE

He flew over half the earth
just to be with her
swaying gently
in the ebb and flow of the Pacific Ocean
watching the sunrises and sunsets

MODERN ART MUSEUM

In the Modern Art Museum
thin dust on the board
is the most vulnerable

Tiny waves on the lake
are the most heart-touching

Twinkling stars in the night sky
are the most fascinating

But her faint reflection on the window
is her unspoken longing

PICTURE OF A ROSE

Many people have visited you
a delicate red rose
held in his hand behind

But only one person for many years
carved you secretly
in her fragrant mind

COLOR OF OLD MEMORIES

The grey sky paints the little tree
with the color of old memories in grey

WALKING ON THIS TRAIL

You choose to walk on this trail
covered in shimmering white snow

A squirrel is gathering leaves
to prepare for the winter cold

A deer is turning its head
to say Hi before crossing your road

You choose to walk on this trail
in white snow leading to the unknown

A STANDING TREE

Written by my daughter Katie

Leaves rustling in the soft wind
but still, he stands firm
Rain threatens the earth
but still, he stands strong
Firm he stays, until the end
of his life, which may be many years
And so he stays for all his life
standing there, unmoving, and still

At last, he is too weak to stand
the wind still blows, the leaves still
Rustle, the rain still falls
These will continue, but he will not
for the time has come, and he will go
The wind will blow, and the rain will fall
a new tree will come, grow tall and strong
He will stand firm
against these winds and rains
Until just like the other
he will fall, the same

The wind still blows
the rain still falls
New trees grow

old trees fall
This will continue until the end of the world
until the wind stops blowing
and the rain stops falling

A LITTLE TREE UNDER CLOUDS

A little tree under white clouds
still dreams to lift his sky into the white clouds

A RED CARDINAL

"Who heard the snow falling last night?"

"Me, Me, Me. I stopped by your window last
night."

Answered the red cardinal

BRIDGE IN SNOW

Snowflakes fall gently
hugging the bridge into its warmth

Snowflakes fall quietly
Listening to the creek of time and space

RED LEAVES

It is a beautiful day after snow
Frost paints on the leaves
The big and small "zeros"
Coloring the branches
With deep and shallow red shades

ICY RAIN

Stars fall from the sky
in a peaceful night
dancing on the branches
like icy butterflies

LONELY SNOWMAN

The lonely snowman thought himself
the loneliest soul in the icy cold

he didn't notice the little jade lion
looking at him sadly from behind

ICY LAKE HEART

How many seasons must pass
Spring Summer Autumn and Winter?

How many footsteps must walk
shallow and deep on a snowy lake

to get closer and closer
to your warm heart
sealed in the icy cold?

REALIZATION

Walking in the circles of footprints
the snowman realized in later years
he was already in the place to find his peace of mind

SNOW IN THE VILLAGE

Furry snow of white
falling from the sky
dances in a winter night
to hug the pebbles in the creek

Furry snow of white
sings with the whispers of the poet
to put sweet dreams in us
of the spring flowers at the oceanside

DUCKY IN SNOW

Too little to take an adventure on her own
the little girl paints a ducky playing in snow
who has the courage to explore the world unknown

A TIN TOY SOLDIER IN SNOW

"Are you feeling cold, tin soldier in snow?"

"Yes. It is cold, I still wait for her as she would know."

BLUE ROBE OF LIGHT

The tree in the blue robe of light
expresses his endless love
for the azure starry sky at night

A TINY SNOWBALL

Snow curls into a tiny snowball
sleeping in the shallow footprint
on the white snow just fallen